In Ghostlight

Southern Messenger Poets

Dave Smith, Series Editor

In
Ghostlight

poems

Ryan Wilson

LOUISIANA STATE UNIVERSITY PRESS ▐▌ BATON ROUGE

Published by Louisiana State University Press
lsupress.org

LSU PRESS PAPERBACK ORIGINAL

DESIGNER: Mandy McDonald Scallan
TYPEFACE: Fournier MT Pro

COVER IMAGE: *The Home of the Heron*, by George Inness, 1893.
Courtesy of the Art Institute of Chicago.

Cataloging-in-Publication Data are available at the Library of Congress.

ISBN 978-0-8071-8129-4 (paperback) | ISBN 978-0-8071-8147-8 (epub)
ISBN 978-0-8071-8148-5 (pdf)

A.M.D.G.

for Matthew Buckley Smith

. . . we live by an invisible sun within us.

—SIR THOMAS BROWNE

The power of the memory is prodigious, my
God. It is a vast, immeasurable sanctuary. Who
can plumb its depths? And yet it is a faculty of
my soul. Although it is part of my nature, I can-
not understand all that I am. This means, then,
that the mind is too narrow to contain itself
entirely. But where is that part of it which it does
not itself contain? Is it somewhere outside itself
and not within it? How, then, can it be part of
it, if it is not contained in it? I am lost in wonder
when I consider this problem. It bewilders me.

—ST. AUGUSTINE, *CONFESSIONS, BOOK* X

I saw eternity the other night,
Like a great ring of pure and endless light . . .

—HENRY VAUGHAN, "THE WORLD"

And the light shineth in the darkness; and the
darkness comprehended it not.

—JOHN 1.5

Contents

In Ghostlight

The Call

Buried, at three, in quilts and pillows, I
Heard grown-up voices coming through the wall
Quietly, and tall stars nailed night to the sky
Beyond my window, and my world, where all
Was darkness and the bony hands of trees
Reaching out through the marbled earth like men
Interred before their time, desperate to seize,
With starving lungs, the fire of breath again.

My brother slept beside me like the dead.
I tossed, turned. Spiraling into my sleep,
I heard coyotes howl, and sat up in bed,
My mind unfenced, and freed from leaping sheep,
Then rose, to seek what I could not possess,
Life howling through the dark hills' wilderness.

Heorot

It is creeping across

    the withered backcountry.

Where grim fogs graze hills

    and gray mists haunt

the hollows that hug

    our forsaken highways,

it lurches through thickets,

    downs leaves, downs limbs.

It strips the bronze stalks

    of the harvest, it steals

the firstling of the flock

    to gladden its feeding.

In a ditch by our fence

    they found Doc's daughter.

The balefires burn.

    Others are butchered.

Groped by our grief,

    in the grizzled air

we have shrieked lamentations,

    longing for a law

to punish the predator

    and make firm a peace.

All the high councils

    have condemned the creature,

and still it stands

    astride the county,

cruel as winter,

    the cold's own kinsman.

The nightly news

    repeats its nothing;

our Facebook friends

    cry wolf, unfollow us.

It shakes its iron

       shackles in the shadows,

it rattles its wrench

       over the roof gables,

in the darkness outside

       our doors, it dances,

and will not wander

       from the farms it has wasted,

the monstrous changeling,

       unchosen, our child.

November 2016

The Birth of Tragedy

Funny story. I wasn't able to walk upright on my own
Two too long before I found myself possessed by an urge to go
       outside and play.
One rule: stay, stay in the yard. So I'd twirl myself dizzy and fall,
       lisp "Highway to the Danger Zone,"
Roll down the hill like a barrel, or teeter clapping at lightning bugs.
       But in the yard I'd stay.
What a good boy am I! I'd think. (Jack Horner was good, not mean
       like that snot Georgie Porgie).
Then one day the sky was wolves and the faraway pines were smoky
       and I was bad and alone.
At first, my wooden rifle blew bad men without faces to smithereens
       in a petulant orgy
Of deathless death. And then I saw the farmhouse down the road by
       the pines. Then I was gone.

October, and the field wild with broom and tares was a harmonious
       bronze sea, enwoven
With quick patterns by slithering winds. I stumbled toward the happy
       white house on the remote
Hilltop, brandishing my toy. Arriving, though, I found porch steps
       broken, windows missing, and darkness inside. Sensing a
       coven
Of witches might be in there waiting, watching, I scared, turned. *Baaa!*
       Face to face with a goat,
I leapt from the porch and made the dirt road, running all the way home
       and filling the gray sky
With shrieking and terror, the goat chasing, and tears, and no one could
       hear me or help me not die.

Field Work

A *post-hole digger*. Heavens, just how tightly
    Can sounds enclose a thing, penning it
Into a function that—wrongly or rightly—
    Isolates it from the infinite
And nameless stuff of possibility,
       Driving it down in the hard ground of Time?
          Sky-minded Summer, and for three whole days
The old man never says a word to me
    As we repeat work's ancient paradigm
       Over and over in the August blaze.

What we were making was a phantom fence.
    From the night woods, wild things come to possess
The fields they've lost to human violence
    And savvy, as the dark itself returns to bless
The troubled mind with sleep. Then, herds of deer,
    Shy as dreams, graze the rows day's labor made
       And woodchucks gorge themselves on cabbages;
The ghostly bobcat and the fox appear,
    And timber rattlers, cooling in the shade,
       Unfold like the nightmare that history is.

It was to keep them out, as best we could,
    And to protect the body's nourishment,
We worked against that spectral brotherhood
    Which summons us back to that place we went
Forth from, the reeling center where the prey
    And predator move together in a dance
       Like lovers, knowing neither fear nor rage,
Seeing what is, without the shadow-play
    Of mind, that place which is our provenance
       On earth, and is our earthly heritage.

Six feet apart, a grave's depth, we dug holes
    Around the field, leaving dirt piles behind
Us as if we were really tunneling moles
    Building a darkling home, our workings blind.
But then came posts, and then the fence's wire.
    A shape emerged. Until our fingers numbed,
        We fastened lengths of fence wire to the wood,
Stretching it tight till, like some antique lyre,
    When plucked by the high winds the whole fence hummed.
        The task complete, the old man grinned, said "Good

Enough." It was, and wasn't. So things go.
    The fence stood twenty years, though you did not,
Grandfather. And I know now I can't know
    More than a few odd stories of your lot
In life. You rarely spoke about your past—
    That drunken brute, your father—or The War.
        Today the field is scrub pine and broom sedge.
Within the green walls you were pent at last,
    As was your work, and what you did it for.
        Still, nights, I sense you coming to the edge

Of consciousness with those dark ministers
    Of the forgotten you strove to keep out,
And hear, within the crickets' pulsing whirrs,
    Your endless silence like a voiceless shout
Imploring me with I-can't-understand-
    What motive to do something different:
        To spare no pains, and to spare no cost
But make whatever work comes from my hand
    Summon the quick back to that place we went
        Forth from, and welcome back from there the lost.

Sharecroppers

They did their work, and they were strong enough.
They plucked all morning, and all afternoon,
Prizing from thorns a blizzard of soft stuff
That brought them bread until the Hunter's moon
Called them away from homes they held on loan,
And days in fields of light they didn't own.

Unknown in life—the fog of generations
Obscures my people now, dark silhouettes
Looming, enormous, in imagination's
Unearthly fields, where what the land forgets
Persists. Faceless, they go on, the forgotten
Whose blood is mine, whose name is my own name,
In radiant ghostlight, still picking cotton.
I join them now, on whom Time has no claim.

Philoctetes, Long Afterward

They're nice to me, I guess,
These ghosts who never quite know what to say,
Having lived out meaningless
Lives here in Thessaly. They fear each day
That they have been somehow defrauded,
But bring me my Dilaudid
Out on this sunny terrace anyway

In their soft shoes and scrubs.
They putter forward into their futures while
Helping us into tubs
Or pushing Lethean pills to coax a smile
From us, who see, played on these plains
Once more, our ancient pains,
The green a stage that holds Troy's burning pile.

It's like some movie set,
This hospice. We're the actors; they're the crew.
They bring our Percocet
And coffee, do the lights. What do we do?
We act like we are still the men
We were, in that time when
Our lives still mattered. Could be worse. It's true

Time's poison ravages
The body, but what are gout and diabetes
To one who knows what he is,
What he was? What can they be to Philoctetes?
I am the man who slaughtered Paris
For his crime, here, on a terrace
In a wheelchair, dribbling milk from soggy Wheaties,

browbeaten by these ghosts
Who've never lived. Here's the survivor's fate.
        And always with the ghosts . . .
My own dead friend came to equivocate
        For Pyrrhus and Odysseus,
        And he made such a fuss
That I slouched off to fight for men I hate.

        For what? Lo! My reward
For saving the Achaeans with my bow?
        Great Agamemnon, Lord
Of Men, long dead; Achilles, too, laid low,
        And no one cares what they debated
        Or how, manipulated,
I left where Lemnos' sleepy breezes blow

        As soft as Mother Peace
Upon the fevered brow of her sick child,
        Who's sick with the disease
Of life. They could have left me in the wild
        Where I'd hobble from my quiet cave
        Like Lazarus from the grave,
My dying and my living reconciled

        As in some afterlife
I could not end, since ending it would mean
        Another afterlife.
I've never seen such darkly brilliant green . . .
        Living on bread the ravens brought
        And the few fish I caught . . .
Things I'd ignored for years took on the sheen

Of jeweled seas at noon,
The deep-down stir of things made evident
While I lay in a swoon
On a stone ledge above the forest, bent
Over a sprig of thyme, white-capped,
As if some breaker lapped
Within the limestone shelf its growth had rent.

The changeful days were changeless,
And I was most alive when numbered dead,
When the unexpected angels
Of daily observation crowned my head
As mayflies form a halo over
A lily in the clover
Nobody's ever seen. But now, instead

Of that, the TV blares,
I e-mail different people. Memory fades.
We're dying. No one cares.
They feed us burnt steaks. We wield plastic blades,
And wish we'd known the naïve joy
Of those love felled at Troy,
Who don't now live as shades among the shades.

A Haunted House

A hush of wind came with us
Through the door and,
In the forsaken room
Where we stood
Silent amid the years
Of dust and cobwebs,
Sent the dry leaves skittering
On the unswept floor.
Just ordinary ruin, nothing
More: plate garnished
With a bug's integument,
A table, chairs
Some furious event
Long quiet
Overturned,
Dead bird
In a drawer.

We felt, outside,
The dearth of words
To say. We, who were
Young, preoccupied
With sex, on our
Vacation, felt
Time's rusty knife pressed
To our throats,
And then we walked away.
We've lost touch, now,
But the wind's hush recollects
That day's happenings,
The happiness of that life.

For a Dog

You'd wake us up—that shrill, insistent bark
Driving away whatever dreams had fogged
Our vision—and we'd rise in the true dark,

Wondering just what exactly, catalogued
By canine instinct under "THREAT," was there,
What jogger, cat, or dog it was that dogged

You from your drowse beside the easy chair
And summoned your yapped pandemonium.
Nine times in ten it was just empty air,

Some ghosted scent you sniffed. Dumb—you were dumb,
Like all dogs, snuffling up to snakes, afraid
Of mice. When we said "come," you wouldn't come;

You capered when commanded to play dead,
And when we wanted most to be alone
You'd offer up that imbecilic head

Until we crowned your pity with a bone.
Our lives took on the shape you spun from need,
The harried rondure of routine. You gone,

The house is quieter, and we've been freed
Forever from the never-ending chores
Your tail entailed, the scrubbing where you peed,

The hunting stain removers down in stores.
What's hardest are the peaceful hours we wanted
So much when you were scratching up the doors

And howling at some phantom thing that haunted
The world without, some threat we couldn't see
That you were desperate to have confronted.

Now you're part of that present unity
Of absences the living move among,
In which what was, what will, and what can't be

Dance in a ring to a triumphant song
We don't have ears to hear, or heart to see,
Who sleep now perfectly, and much too long.

i.m. Achates Baudelaire

Behind the Music

What? What is this, unhappy Orpheus,
This madness that's undone both you and me?
—Vergil, *Geo.* iv. 494–95

The Maenads were another story.
    Only blank years could wear
Away the otherworldly glory
    He'd dreamed. Only despair

Could tame that wild tongue with the truth.
    Even with her in Hades,
He'd spritz his vodka with vermouth
    And let drinks conjure ladies

Sprawling before him, fawning over
    The *brave*, the *sensitive*
Genius who'd stormed Hell for his lover.
    Dreams are one way to live.

So. One night he typed out a dream:
    Great loss, he knew, needs closure.
To say he'd been ripped limb from limb
    Resolved into composure

What otherwise was open-ended:
    It calmed the sea to glass,
One might say. Well, it was too splendid
    A lie, shriller than brass

In broad sun, but he knew the tale
    Would be loved, being easy
Enough to pacify love's failures.
    Alive, he hid in sleazy,

All-night dives, downing martinis
      Alone in the timeless dark,
Got old while lithe girls in bikinis
      Lay tanning in the park

With rich tech-kids who'd never heard
      Of him, or his doomed passion,
Got older when he learned the word
      Itself was out of fashion,

And yet lived, crooked, drunk, and hoary,
      Beyond the nameless pain
He'd known, beyond his dream of glory,
      An ancient man made sane

By senselessness. In his last weeks,
      He wrote, much to his credit,
A song through which the sad truth speaks
      Cleanly. Few have read it.

Hesperides

She's got her magazine, he's got his Scotch.
The rain drums its fingertips idly on the roof.
Some sitcom's laugh-track cackles. They don't watch.
Don't hear, don't speak. It's late. They've had enough
Communion with themselves, each in a chair
On either side of the living room tonight,
As every night, each offering a dead stare
Like a sacrifice to the opposite wall's white:
White sun, white sand, white clouds in tropic skies . . .
And: *Moonlight on white flesh in youth's faraway pond.* . . .
A long-haul trucker's fist rubs sleep-fogged eyes
That glimpse a porchlight in the dark beyond
The highway: the farmhouse, where two sit, mute,
Hangs far in the unknown night its golden fruit.

Lemons

Hell getting here. Roads serpentine squiggles wriggling through
      jagged mountains toward the green
Valley of Vesuvius' shadow, apocalyptic traffic by Naples, hairpin
      turns on nightmare drops above
That sea Horace once watched polish the cliffs two thousand and
      fifty years ago, guessing the scene
Meant we should take our days in hand like grapes, metacarpals on
      their waxy surface delicate as first love.
Keats, who plagiarized Horace, wished, dying, he could burst joy's
      grape against his palate fine,
Trusting, I guess, inside every day's fragile membrane was a juice
      like joy. Then that sublime
Weirdo, Hopkins, asked "What is all this juice and all this joy?"
      Great poems. But they're not mine.
Here in Sorrento, in the ruin of my life, I sit, scribbling, in the shadows
      of the lemon trees, smelling the cold purple smell of Time.

It smells like stone, like minerals, like horses galloping through a green
      field oblivious of the fences.
The sea Etruscans saw shimmers in the moonlight like asphalt on empty
      Georgia highways at noon.
There is a dark hallway, in which each door is locked, that one reaches
      by the stairway of the senses,
And it goes on forever, door after door. Waiting here, I'm tempted to
      think one might open soon
And I might cross the threshold of the mystery. Waiting, I see lemons
      hanging in the summer heat
Like Chinese lanterns on an endless pathway through the woods, like the
      warmly glowing golden windows of lit rooms on a winter's
      midnight street.

Days

Snow over everything. Snow over cars
And roads and lawns, snow mounding the mailboxes:

Undesecrated moonscape. It's so clear,
This dawn. Soon we will excavate rushed lives,

Spring into threadbare costumes and perform
Our duties like those one-hit wonders still

Crooning in ever-smaller dives of soon-
To-be-ghost-towns beloved tunes they hate,

Foul darkness crowding, no clock on the walls.
Nobody ever wants to hear the new stuff.

Bowls and cups on our tables wait, expectant.
Young, I went chasing after fame, or wished,

At least, my words might not go unremembered.
My sole wish, now, is to go back, back South,

Back where I come from, walk the gravel roads
And summer fields again, people so scarce

The area is unincorporated,
Pale clouds like sails in the blue swim of boyhood skies,

And come again at last to that grove in the pines
Where an entire small family lies buried

In purple shadows and strewn golden straw,
Simple white marble for the father and mother,

And round about them smaller stones, a few
No more than common rocks, nameless, dateless.

II. LINES NEARING THE SPRING EQUINOX

Touches of warmth swim through the hollow cold,
A goldleaf school of bream too small to eat,

Bic lighters deep in the Korykian Cave.
Life glimmers in the green eyes of the grass,

The hazel eyes that wear that far-off look.
It's time to gather up all my belongings

And lay them down in boxes, bury them—
Keepsakes and prized books—in the echoing

Mausoleum of a moving truck.
Moving! Already in the distant hills

Among the wildwoods and the rusted farms
An empty place awaits me and my burdens,

A place beside a lake where I can fish
For poems drifting through the dazzled silence.

Still, like a spoiled brat, now with my gray beard
I boohoo and a few tears glaze this face

Passing through rooms I will not see again,
Except in glimpses, through the radical dark

Of dreams. How many ghostlives must one leave
Behind in life's meanderings through earth?

The infant jonquils, hesitatingly,
Dip their jade brush-tips in a pot of sunshine.

III. SUMMER NIGHT

Thunder breaks something huge and goes off grumbling
Around the night's horizons. Intervals,

Anxious, are filled with an orchestral green:
The frogs and crickets keep time in the dark

Like consciousness. I am a troubled child
Who has not been a child for thirty years.

A candid photograph of lightning catches
Wind whipping bearded wheatfields into waves.

Cups and plates clatter in the kitchen cupboard.
Voile curtains lift and fall in quiet bedrooms.

What secrets cause them to keep arguing,
Heaven and earth, like separated parents

Pulling our hearts in two with fears and hopes?
When will a bashful rain come ease this tension?

Must we repeat the same lines? Scenes? A troupe
Of muddied actors, everywhere we go

All our lives long? A thousand miles away
From boyhood and the same storm threatening,

I think of watercourses with white hair
Wandering down their rocky mountainsides.

Crickets and frogs. Ghost moonlight peeks between
Purple cloudfingers covering its face.

IV. SEPTEMBER

Some flunkies from the faceless government
Have paved the dirt road over. Glossy cars

Go hissing past anonymous as wind.
The cornfield's overgrown with worthless vetch.

There are no neighbors swaying on wide porches
As they once did, wheat ears in a blue breeze.

It's twenty years since I last came back home.
The nearby houses sag, bleared clapboard ruins.

Kings now, stout crows sit throned atop the bowing
Telephone poles. Crazed wires score mute gray skies.

Gone is the green ogive the live oaks lofted
Above the farmhouse, molting now, crouched small

In tall brown grasses like a wounded hare
This autumn. Gone the weathered gable barn

With its tin roof, where in the secret dark
Of childhood I would trace my fingertips

Slowly across the rough mystery of iron
Tools older than any world my thoughts could hold.

We go blind, dazzled in the swim of days,
Unless loss teach the soul to see all's strange.

Clumps of scrub pine possess old garden plots.
Our trellis for the muscadine stoops down

Now, overgrown with honeysuckle, still
In bloom despite the cool. Soon I will go.

As in boyhood, I pluck a silky blossom,
Yellow as an old photograph, and, chilled

Breathe deep the sicksweet, selfless smell of change.

Windy October Night, Waterside

Lève l'ancre pour une exotique nature!
—Mallarmé

Abandoned yachts, and less immoderate skiffs,
Resigned in their rope webbing
To the harbor's sulfide reek, still softly rock
In starlit flooding and ebbing
Tonight, and sometimes, like age's vague what-ifs,
Rise toward the rickety dock

(Which holds them restless captives far too often)
On a poor excuse for a wave
And give a hollow knock, a wooden sound,
The thud of a man in his grave
Awakening and pounding on his coffin
Uselessly. Think of the drowned

Anchors that smile now in the sediment
Of what's forever lost.
Think of the toilet seats the hydrophytes
Have purfled and embossed
With Byzantine designs, the fortune spent,
In coins, on wishes, nights

Like this, the rods fish caught, the rusting hulls
Of pleasure's swift excesses,
The steel-toe boots, their laces undulating
Like Ophelia's loosened tresses,
The grace of slow decomposition, skulls
Of lovers done debating

Hope's chance, the jetsam of our sunlit days
      All gathered, now, together
In a realm where the celestial bodies seem,
      Themselves, tenants, and weather
Means nothing. All that is eternally sways
      In the green dark of a dream . . .

The night-wind lifts. With wavelets' supple plashes
      The creaks of straining ropes,
Like old doors opening or closing, augur
      The coming of fresh hopes.
So why should food forever smack of ashes?
      You swig your trendy lager.

If loss, like logic, holds as axiom
      That life is misery,
The membrane separating you from God's
      The present tense of *be*.
So why trudge through the decades yet to come,
      The bleak Iditarods

Of your tomorrows, glacial grind of years,
      When their brute apparatus
Of frostbite, wolves, snow-blindness, and despair
      Conspires to keep, as *status*
Quo, your face bejeweled with frozen tears?
      To leave, to go out there,

To enter the eternal world of myth
        Is simple. Just stop being.
As soon as your few friends lose their last thought
        Of you (which will prove freeing
For them) you'll find yourself among, forthwith,
        The Deathless Things you've sought.

In that subaqueous glow the deep world must
        Think rises and illumines
The vacant moon, perhaps the skeletons
        Wish peace upon us humans,
Who fog our world with hopeful clouds of dust,
        Us wild-eyed, anxious ones,

Who hear our deathless parts, *souls* if you will,
        Like children locked in a closet,
Pounding the door, pleading to be released.
        Perhaps, if one may posit
A bold conjecture, we must learn to kill
        Ourselves, or kill, at least,

What ties us to the world, that we may know
        The peace of innocence,
Cool as a breeze through a hole in the smoky cortex.
        It's starting to make some sense . . .
(Jump off the dock. Jump. Jump! . . .) No, not yet. No.
        The whirling silken vortex

Tomorrow promises is easier
        Than passing through life's portal,
Somehow. Two deaths diverge in every wood,
        And you, you must be mortal,
And die the slow death others would prefer.
        Let's call that love. Yeah? Good.

(Of course, we're kept alive by cowardice,
        But let's not say such things.
For God's sake, there are children: grow some pity!)
        Think of the sufferings
That, missing you, shattered some stranger's bliss.
        Now, turn to the glittering city

Behind you. Walk back down the dock (and note
        That you're so fortunate
To walk) and see, with your own blessèd vision,
        The world you might have quit,
That sloping bank, dark tree-line, those remote
        Skyscrapers. Make the decision

To walk the streets again, to be distracted.
        There, lovers flirt, nonstop,
And money's made. Don't notice the lamppost
        (Filigreed iron, its top
Flowering) to which the moths are so attracted
        Houses an eager host

Who's tidying his home, making exquisite
        Baroque designs for all
The wingèd things whose maddened little flight
        Might lead them, soon, to call
On him by chance, or error. Don't ask, *Is it*
        For all who seek the light?

The Feast of the Epiphany

Hard going, yes, for an astronomer,
A man of science, the cold journey long.
Especially for three such as we were:
Scatterbrains, mooncalves, heads full of sphere-song,
Kings of forgotten realms (perhaps not extant
For all we knew). Applying esoteric terms
Of azimuths, nuances of the sextant,
To striking tents and goading pachyderms,
We lumbered day and night through desert places,
Incarcerated by pain, hunger, thirst,
Our one hope that hope held, in fact, no basis.
What doesn't kill us only makes us stranger.
Among the oxen, sheep, and pigs, we cursed
Our charts, and stared, lost, starving, at the manger.

Christmas Party

One more dead party, and, off to the side
Among the knickknacks and the curios,
In a blue blazer you assume the pose
Of one whose patterned noose is loosely tied,
Of one belonging here, one clearly meant
For artificial lights and merriment.

The revelers, snug in their ugly sweaters,
Swill booze and bellow their inanities
On weather and the decorated trees
Which, shackled in their brightly colored fetters,
Like those depressives cast in festive roles,
Suggest the straitening of certain souls

By circumstance and expectation's bonds,
Those somber ones who, in Time's echoes reeling,
Can find no word to name their thought or feeling,
No thing with which the spirit corresponds,
But go on going on, keep showing up
To sip punch out of someone else's cup.

Bless them. Bless all the wanderers who move
Through shadowed wastes of memory and desire,
Whose native realm's a fraudulent empire
That slips the grasp like smoke, or hopeless love.
And bless that hallowed world which no names name,
Where we're all citizens, and loved the same.

Into our talk, its emissaries steal
To bring us tidings of what we forget;
Its kingdom holds what's past, and what's not yet;
Its language is the language of the real,
Which we hear, in each momentary pause
In conversation, whispering its laws,

As now, outside, snow whispers to the earth
The secrets of the darkness that's the sky.
Listen. And listen to the earth's reply,
The pregnant silence of that virgin birth
That gives each moment hope, and hears
Us, in a falling blizzard, lift faint *Cheers*.

Re-Entry

Mercury-Atlas 6: 1962

Down from the otherworldly altitudes
Where, body weighing little as a thought,
The buoyant dark holds Artemis aloft
And I shared one perspective with the gods,
Who do and do not care what they have wrought,
I came, the fiery atmospheric shift
Shaking my bones like rocks in a Coke can,
The gimcrack globe no more a glaucous blue
Eye staring into dim infinities
Now but a mouth, and I now ash, dust, man,
My gauges haywire, unsure what was true,
Penetrating the membrane of the skies.
Soon: weddings, Mays, the Beatles, Marilyn's obits,
Kids, supermarkets, dreams of grander orbits.

Next Up

A thousand miles and twenty years away
From you—lightyears, it seems—before my class
Starts, one gusty, early April day

I watch the phalanxes of students pass
Hurrying through spectral clouds of their hot breaths,
Some slapping fives, some reveling in crass

Jokes, others shouting out youth's shibboleths.
Passionate, awkward, silly—as we were—
They rush to "kill" exams, and to their deaths

The way that people do. Days, weeks, months blur.
Hours chase each other round and round the clock,
And years thumb through a lifetime's calendar

Like an old Yellow Pages, just to chuck
It out. Someday, these students may be feeling
What I do now—that mere survival's luck—

Watching the year's first cherry blossoms reeling
Through the Spring's glacial air, pale galaxies'
Revolutions in fast-forward, huge gusts wheeling

Phantom flotillas into maelstrom seas.
Not everyone has had the luck I've had.
I see you and your friends, the fake I.D.s

I got you (and you'd wanted them so bad!).
Lord, you were proud and happy with your beer
At 18. . . . And I see your tough-guy Dad

Weeping beside your coffin the next year.
I glimpse us playing catch, just little kids,
Wincing, Saturday's brush-stroked sky sincere,

Or racing through the twilight katydids'
Pulsing, or stealing off into the woods
To smoke and brag. Whatever age forbids

We sprinted after like earth's only goods.
So young, we dreamed only of being older.
While your Dad, a good man, roofed our neighborhoods,

We couldn't warm to homes where hopes grew colder
With comfort. Friend, you've won the last of races.
Kids older than you ever were now shoulder

Fashionable burdens. Blossoms in our faces
Like ghostly avalanches are cascading,
And there you are, you're twelve, circling the bases

As fast as possible, the bright ball fading
Out of blue sky into dark trees like some
Untutored sun that seeks out its own shading,

Crowd roaring in the moment's astrodome:
Brief hero, sunlight's warmth against your neck,
Springs blossoms fall, it's Summer, you cross home

And reach out for me where I stand on deck.

   i.m. Jay Mills (1984–2003)

Velocities

The spry young sprinter
I once was left me behind
For good this winter

Morning on my jog,
When, my legs gone rubber, a
J. Crew catalogue

Of lithe Apollos
Blithely passed by, then vanished.
I know what follows:

Back pain, ravaged knees,
A cruel accrual of
Mounting maladies

And slow, then slower
Movements, till checking the mail
Means a half hour

Lost, overborne bones
Creaking—old house in high winds—
With the speed of stones

Skipped life bounding past
And blurring into perfect
Stillness far too fast.

Apparition

Horace

Still spoiled, still young, still filthy rich with gifts
That Venus gives, when hopeless Winter drifts
Down on your upturned head, and when your hair,
Now loosely floating down in debonair
Cascades along your shoulders, is all gone,
And when your Renaissance complexion—
Now lovelier than blooming damask roses—
Undergoes a startling metamorphosis
And in the mirror, your once-bright eyes bleared,
You see a haggard visage with a beard,
Each time that stranger in the looking-glass
Appears you'll mutter to yourself, "Alas,
Why didn't I in boyhood, long ago,
Possess a mind that knew what now I know?
Why can't that youth I still feel now replace
What then I scorned, turning away my unspoiled face?"

Vacation

After toweling off from an early swim and breakfast on the lanai—
Eggs Benedict and grapefruit juice with chilled orange slices blotting
       the morning paper—
The brassy sunlight blowing slow and woozy as it did in days gone by,
Those lakeshore Summers filled with rope swings and dockside secrets,
       first loves and lonely kayaks in the moonlight, cookouts and the
       obligatory annual conspiratorial caper
Against one of the oldsters concluding in mild embarrassment, the
       whispered plot always thwarted,
Mothers and fathers inevitably gathered on front lawns to clap and
       laugh at their sheepish children's comeuppance,
Affirming that the youngsters' time was not yet come, that they themselves
       were not so dotty as reported,
I run my fingers across my head grown suddenly bald again and wonder
       how it happens
I'm now as old as they were then. Older, maybe. Our boys are nearly
       grown, and still asleep.
Bless them, they stay up all hours texting girls back home, a thousand
       miles way. My wife
Is reading D. H. Lawrence and says she wants to get a tattoo. She says
       that I'm not "deep,"
And maybe she's right. I do my work (and I do pretty well), keep fit,
       and try to shape this life
Of choice and chance and change into something pleasant. Is it so bad
       to try to be content?
Is it so very dreadful to forgive the world the wounds that it delivers? I
       don't know. . . .

Later on, there will, of course, be storms: it's Florida. Already, strong
    headland winds are bent
Toward us. Gusts send cypressfuls of birds scattering from hiding places.
    Where do they go?
Where do we go? The summer I was seventeen, about a week before I
    had to leave for college,
I woke up around three o'clock and scumbled barefoot through the damp
    grass down to the lake,
The fog so thick I blindly breathed it in. My feet moved almost without
    my knowledge,
Long habit being like a trance, and at the ruined wooden bridge a young
    man—and no mistake—
Came out of nowhere: mid-twenties, unshaven face furious with purpose,
    each fiery eye a star.
Then he was gone. And yet, years later, he loops through memory, an
    earworm whose repetitions go on and on and on.
Yesterday morning a mockingbird came in the sliding door and wouldn't
    leave. It didn't even budge when I used the broom to shoo it out,
    so I gave up and sat down and started browsing some books my
    wife brought on the trip—a bunch of poetry in languages I don't
    understand, but somehow lovely anyway: *Non omnis moriar,*
I mumbled to myself, not knowing what it meant, and *J'ai plus des souvenirs*
    que si j'avais mille ans.

Remembrance

What I remember
Is—dusk or dawn

Of some December
That's now long gone,

Snow thick, and flurries
Wafting, wind-whirled,

The sole stirring that worries
The woods' dead world,

Their Anglo-Saxon
Wrought-iron dark—

That trickster-vixen:
Ghostblaze, her spark

From a thicket's runes rushing
Like wildfire ignites

The icescape and flushing
Shadowbirds lights

That charcoal sketch
Of life aglow;

Peach suntints catch
Flame in the snow,

Green chant the pines,
Then all is lost

But dark tracks, hollowed signs,
Their quick gleaming with frost.

Secrets

I'm not saying that
they're breaking news, though, when
they're news, they sometimes break

their keepers. They're more like beggars
from whose gaze we turn away,
whose human presence we refuse.

Nestled in each darkened house,
like dream-thralled sleepers,
their warm light hid, like lonely fires

that burn in frozen woods, they're often
not the dirty things we love to find
those whom we hate are guilty of. In fact,

you cannot live
beyond the age of twenty-five
or thirty without them. They're what

we withhold from the State, The Internet,
the argumentative. For reasons
we may not recall, they must be

kept, like the bagful of plastic bags,
drawerfuls of knickknacks
Puritans would toss: and so they gather,

patiently as dust on polished silver,
as dusk that slowly drags long shadows
through cornfields, patient as loss,

which finds us out, all of us,
as if we ourselves were something left unspoken,
so precious it's not for buying,

or for selling, the unguessed presents
piled beneath the tree, still waiting
for the miracle. You know, it might be

you don't get them: there's no telling.

The Rain

after Borges

Brusquely the evening that was overcast
Has cleared as steady rain's already falling.
Falling or fallen. Rain is itself a thing
Undoubtedly that happens in the past.

Whoever hears it fall has grasped the dead
Time when the Fates, smiling down in repose,
Revealed to him a flower called *the rose*
And all the curious redness of its red.

This rain which now blinds windows with its curtain
Will, in lost suburbs, give life without stopping
To dark grapes of a vine found on a certain

Patio that does not exist. The sopping
Evening brings me the voice—wished for, denied—
Of my father, who turns back, who's never died.

21st-Century Pastoral

Broken-down tractor gone to rust
Amid a field of high-grown sedge.
November light a whisper's ghost.
A split-rail swallowed by a hedge.

Huge weathered barns with roofs caved in
Drifting through fog's amorphous waves.
Mildewed dressmaker's manikin.
Leaves reeling past the hillside graves.

Small farmhouse choking in the fist
Of leafless vines, porch hosting weeds.
The chill of what does not exist.
Jeweled cobwebs' unbroken creeds.

Fields pocked with unreflecting puddles,
Footpaths eroding in the woods;
Skulls baffled by worms' writhing muddles,
Oblivion wandering neighborhoods.

On cinder blocks, an old sportscar.
Yard full of rattlers, coiled, unseen.
Studio in a city far
Away. A blank white laptop screen.

So, Westward

Across bleak stubble fields,
Above the grizzled beechwoods
Riding the ridge's rising
And falling waves, the vanishing
Sun's tossed a bouquet to the sky,
Peach, damson, lead, and gold.

The East's a ghost of blue.
A full moon, fat and white,
Is hung in webs of silver
Clouds like a spider's egg sac.
There's no more turning back.

I'm going home. So, Westward.
My truck waits up ahead,
How far I couldn't say.

Weary of pet sins' weight,
I do love getting lost.

I love not knowing what
Might happen, letting go
Of schemes and meeting strangers
Who stand there waiting around
Each bend inside of me,
Or just beyond each rise.

And now, a night wind spirits
A maple's hoard of gold
Into scrub brush.

And now,
Feeling the joy grooms feel,
I sense inside me something
Rustling, nodding assent
And rustling as it grows
Tall as any man.

Through furred ears and bedraggled pate,
Through the sockets of my eyes,
Through my long, snowdrift beard,
Through my calloused fingertips
And the frail cage of my ribs,
It grows: so soft, so slow . . .

The germ forever opens,
And, now, it's near complete,
Stretching out toward the horizon
In all directions: bronze spears
Like Spartan phalanxes, no—

An endless field of wheat
That, while wind in the last leaves
Sounds faint ovations, ripens.

Wait

But maybe we would be
Content forevermore
With afternoon cascading
Through windows its clean light
On tabletop and chair,
Perched here, uncertainly,
In peppermint-thick air,
As on life's final shore,
The horizon's bouquet fading
Into the kingdom of night.

The kids roll on the rugs
And cry for sandwiches.
Matrons, richly perfumed,
Excavate their purses.
We all know we're doomed,
All dreaming of the drugs
That will, like Orpheus' verses,
Charm the shades that claim
Whatever ever is,
And soon call every name.

A mighty meaning gleams
Now from the delicate
Acts of each wretched day,
And sweetness seems the fate
Of all life, however brief:
Sweetness beyond belief
In children's knee-scuffed play,
The neighbor scrubbing his car,
Our secret, desperate schemes—
In all things, as they are.

Let us forgive each other.
Let us be quiet and kind.
It all ends, and so soon:
A passing afternoon,
This suffering, God!, this glory.
What we seek here, we find.
There is no other story.

One of Many Centurions

Guilt's funny. Magic, some say. He was kneeling,
Blindfolded. We took turns and, laughing, punched
Him, slapped and punched him, daring him to guess
Our names, a legionary's cloak concealing
His eyes. Like we could see. . . . Silent, he hunched
There: jaws, ribs cracked. We cackled. I confess
We thought him something of a pedascule.
He wasn't like us. Redneck paradoxes
And parables: seeds, fig trees, wheat and chaff.
When backwoods bullies bloodied me in school,
I camouflaged my rage, red as a fox is,
Awaiting my revenge. I couldn't laugh,
Though, seeing him, limbs nailed up, crucified—
Hill dark, blood pouring, his arms open wide.

Wind Advisory

Good Friday, 2020, Baltimore, MD

Gray in a spitting snow the castlework
Skyline of a deserted city looms:
Snaggletooth maw of shadows. Nearby lurk
The crooked rows of crumbling, weathered tombs.

This day is one of high winds and disquiet.
Like pendulums, suspension bridges swing
As, with an oceanic boom, gusts riot
Through emptied streets. The wind's in everything.

Last year's leaves rise like ghosts from out the gutters
And in their fury dance phantasmal reels
To the arhythmic banging of our shutters
And the bleak keening of the sirens' peals.

The branches of longstanding oaks are broken.
The trashcans topple and their filth flocks through
The air on nightmare's wings. The truths we've spoken
In these cyclonic winds are whirled untrue.

What we hide from ourselves always emerges.
There is no cure known for this pestilence.
Inside, we hear approaching dark storm surges,
And doing nothing's now our one defense.

The city sinks into a sea of doubt,
Divided like the halves of the *Titanic*.
Everyone's power keeps on going out.
The infected air's electrified with panic.

In fear, some people fight, and some retreat,
But how to beat what we can't see is there?
Drive far away, Death rides in the back seat;
Stay home, and hear Death's footfalls on the stair.

What separates the living and the dead
Is disappearing. May the darkness show
Again tonight the old stars overhead,
Though dogwood petals mingle now with snow.

Disobedience

Piazza San Marco

Here at the labyrinth's heart, I find the air
Is scintillant, just like the postcards show:
A dream of light and strict geometries.
Where the lagoon's receded from the square
Gray stones are dazzled with a blinding glow,
And crowds wait, wincing, in the shimmer's frieze

Like marble waiting for some word or spell
To conjure limbs to life from lifeless stasis,
Or nomads, stunned to find a sudden well
Amid the endless sands, or an oasis.

I feel it. Nightly angst, ennui, and gloom
Refine the human need for some perfection,
Some otherwhere outside routine's dark delves,
And here we are in "Europe's drawing room,"
Napoleon's choicest spot. Sun-glare's reflection
In café windows, we can't see ourselves

At all, which is, I guess, why we worked out
Ways to scrounge up the cash, made plans, and took
The flights. We've dreamed the us we've dreamed about
Awaits us here. But no, not here. See, look:

Campanile cracked, Venetians flee en masse.
The ones stuck here hawk trinkets. For a coin
Tourists go chattering by St. Mark's bones,
And maybe stop a second, as they pass,
Thinking of their rivals back home in Des Moines,
To snap some well-posed selfies with their phones.

Outside, a blizzard of chivalric white,
The seagulls swarm, whirling in clean white air,
And then descend, like jagged shards of light,
To peck to death a pigeon in the square,

Removing flesh until, pink as a tongue,
The innards show. The passersby ignore
The wound, the bird. But there's a girl with bread,
One not too busy being rich or young,
Crouched in the square, small, casting morsels for
The living ones. A saint, I almost said—

It is illegal here to feed a pigeon,
Yet she does, quietly, sure that the law,
Which holds the bottom line's the true religion,
Shall not expunge this world's dark, wingèd flaw.

The Problem

Some grouse, some rattle ice in stormy cocktails, some read, or
      stare into their hands' artificial glow.
The good-natured, whom no one likes, make conversation. Kids
      kick seatbacks; babies scream.
This is the part where you find out exactly who you are, as much
      as you will ever know,
Crammed like seeds into this invaluable lemon with all the dreamed
      escapes you cannot help but dream.
There's something wrong, some unspecified glitch, but nobody will
      say just what it is
Keeping you stranded among strangers here on the hot tarmac, waiting,
Waiting for some pronouncement, some true words that will explain your
      prolonged absences
From the air above the clouds, from flight, from the ocean-front destination
      everyone's anticipating.

It will not last forever, your time on the ground. At some point there will
      come a departure.
Then clouded skies will recede like sunshine, like questions, like your
      toddler's sticky touch, and you will be
Wholly invisible to the earthlings you love, who love you, an arrow shot
      by some blind archer
Beyond the endless traffic and grocery-store pharmacy lines, long-distance
      calls and doctors wincing thoughtlessly.
For now, take solace in the presence of the known world's flawed,
      forgettable, flightless things;
Bless the engine's troubled heart, the brief and inexplicably beautiful problem
      with the wings.

for M.

Acknowledgments and Dedications

Sincere thanks to Mike Aquilina, John Wall Barger, Geoffrey Brock, George David Clark, Alfred Corn, Armen Davoudian, Caitlin Doyle, David Ferry, Piero Filpi, John Foy, Gregory Fraser, Dana Gioia, J. P. Grasser, R. S. Gwynn, Rachel Hadas, Ernest Hilbert, Mark Jarman, Rodney Jones, Shane McCrae, Charles Martin, Robert Pinsky, Brendan Rabon, Chelsea Rathburn, Robert B. Shaw, A. E. Stallings, Daniel Tobin, and James Matthew Wilson. Special thanks to Austin Allen, Fred Chappell, Brad Leithauser, Grace Schulman, Ernest Suarez, Rosanna Warren, and David Yezzi. Above all, thanks to Christopher Childers, Dave Smith, Matthew Buckley Smith, and to my mother, Martha Wilson. Finally, I'm grateful to the editors of the following periodicals, in which many of these poems have previously appeared, sometimes in a slightly different form:

32 Poems: "Wind Advisory"; *American Journal of Poetry:* "Re-Entry"; *Beltway Poetry Quarterly:* "The Wait"; *Birmingham Poetry Review:* "Lemons" and "Next Up"; *The Classical Outlook:* "Hesperides"; *The Dark Horse:* "A Haunted House"; *Evangelization and Culture:* "One of Many Centurions"; *First Things:* "Christmas Party"; *Five Points:* "Behind the Music"; *The Hopkins Review:* "Philoctetes, Long Afterward" and "Windy October Night, Waterside"; *Image:* "Field Work" and "Vacation"; *Literary Imagination:* "Days": *Modern Age:* "Disobedience" and "The Feast of the Epiphany"; *The New Criterion:* "Remembrance"; *Quarterly West:* "The Call"; *The Sewanee Review:* "Heorot," "The Birth of Tragedy," "Velocities," "Sharecroppers," and "The Problem"; *The Yale Review:* "For a Dog."

"21st-Century Pastoral" was first published in the *Plume Poetry 9;* "Heorot" and "For a Dog" were reprinted by *Poetry Daily;* and "For a Dog" appeared previously in *The Stranger World* (2017).

"The Feast of the Epiphany" is for Mike Aquilina.

"Re-Entry" is for Ernest Hilbert.

"Velocities" is for Brad Leithauser.

"Remembrance" is for Kate Robinson.

"One of Many Centurions" is for Dana Gioia.

Printed in the USA
CPSIA information can be obtained
at www.ICGtesting.com
CBHW030201230524
8864CB00022BA/112